Contents

1975   1950

It will soon be Christmas.

At school, we have made angels,
stockings, a Father Christmas
and a snowman.

On the last day of term, we have a party.
Everybody comes in fancy-dress.

We give presents to Father Christmas
to give to poor children.

All the mums
and dads come
and join in
the carol singing.

1975

1950

At home,
we set up the nativity.

We decorate
our Christmas tree.

Mum hangs a wreath
of leaves and berries
on the front door.

54

We make
Christmas cards
to send
to our friends
and wrap up
their presents.

We help Mum
decorate
a gingerbread
house.

1975   1950

Every day, we take turns to open
a door of our advent calendar.

On Christmas Eve,
we hang up our stockings
for Father Christmas.

Look what he brings us!

On Christmas Day, we go to granny's house for Christmas lunch.
All our cousins are there.

We give out our presents . . .

and open our own.

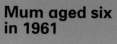
We asked Mum what Christmas was like when she was a little girl.

She said,

'We decorated the house from top to bottom.'

'I made angels from wooden clothes pegs. They had doily dresses and golden wings.'

'We had a silver Christmas tree and a baby Jesus made from plaster.'

10

'Mum made all the Christmas food. I helped her make mince pies.'

'We chose some of our presents from a mail order catalogue.'

'I covered little boxes or made pomanders for my aunts.'

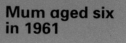

We asked Mum what she did at school before Christmas.

She said,

'We sat at long tables and made Christmas presents. We sewed pin cushions and made decorated calendars.'

'There was always a nativity play. One year, I was the Virgin Mary. I used my doll as baby Jesus.'

'We had a carol service in the church. Our parents came to listen.'

'On the first day
of the school holidays,
Mum took us to see
Father Christmas.
He had a grotto
in one of the big shops.'

'We looked at all the toys
and saw the Christmas lights
hung across the streets.'

13

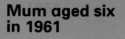
We asked Mum what happened on Christmas Day.

She said,

'I used one of
my dad's thick socks
as a Christmas stocking.
It was always filled
with little toys
and had an orange
in the toe.'

'On Christmas morning,
we opened the last door
of the advent calendar.'

'We went to church.
I loved going to see
the nativity.'

14

Mum said,

'My granny came on Christmas morning. We weren't allowed to open our presents until she had arrived.'

'Our mum and dad often made us presents. One year, Dad made us a doll's house.'

'Mum knitted me a teddy.'

'We were always given a new game and sometimes a kit for making things.'

We asked Mum what her family ate at Christmas.

She said,

'We ate turkey with bread sauce,
sprouts and carrots for lunch.
Then we had
a home-made Christmas pudding.'

'My mum put a sixpence
inside it.
Whoever got it
would be lucky all year.'

'After lunch,
we watched
the Queen's speech
on TV.'

'On Boxing Day, we always went
to see a pantomime.
We dressed in our best clothes.
I wore a velvet dress
and black shiny shoes.'

'One year, we saw Cinderella.'

Granny now

1975   1950

When we asked Granny what she remembered
about Christmas, she said,

'On Christmas Eve, we carried the Christmas tree home.'

'We decorated it with
glass balls, tinsel
and real candles
in tin holders.'

'We also decorated the house
with holly and paper chains,
which we cut and glued ourselves.'

1925   1900

'I hung my stocking
by the fireplace
on Christmas Eve.'

'On Christmas morning,
there was always an apple,
a penny, an orange
and a little book in it.'

'I didn't get many other presents.
I was usually given an annual and
perhaps a skipping rope or a money box .'

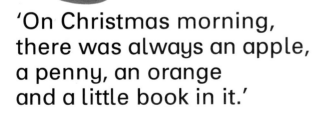

1975   1950

Granny said,

'My mother curled my hair
like Shirley Temple
for Christmas Day.
I hated it.'

'After church, my uncles
and aunts came for lunch.'

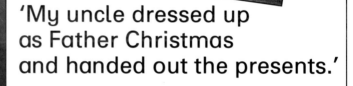

'My uncle dressed up
as Father Christmas
and handed out the presents.'

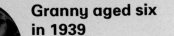

'Then everyone listened
to the King's speech
on the radio or went to sleep.'

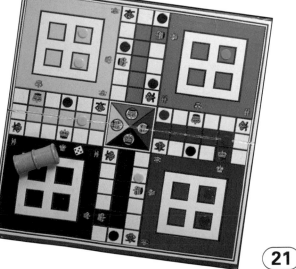

'We children had to play
quiet games.
That was very boring.'

1975   1950

Granny said,

'When I was young, there was a war
between Germany and England.
People couldn't celebrate Christmas
as they normally did.'

PURE DRIED
WHOLE
EGGS
U.S.A

THIS
PACKAGE
CONTAINS

12
EGGS

IN
POWDER FORM

5 OUNCES NET WEIGHT
EQUAL TO 12 EGGS

'There was a shortage of certain foods.
My mother made Christmas pudding
with dried eggs instead of real ones.'

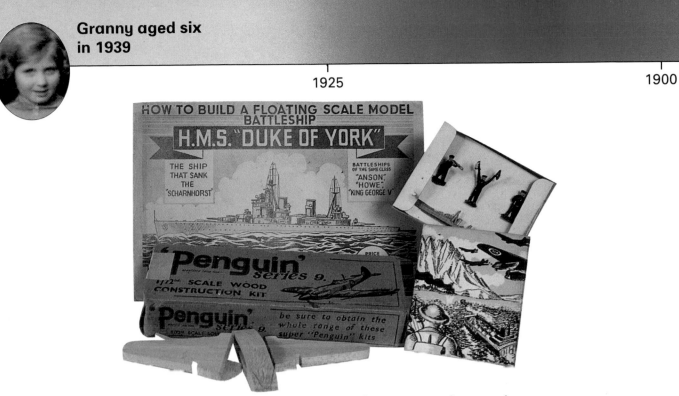

'There weren't many toys around for people to buy.
My mother knitted doll's clothes from odd scraps of wool.
Boys were given war toys.'

'Some children
from towns
were sent to
the country to keep
them safe from bombs.
They went to
a big party
to cheer them up.'

23

1975   1950

We asked Great-granny what Christmas
was like when she was a child.

She said,

'Christmas Day wasn't as big
a celebration as it is nowadays.
A lot of people had to work.
My father drove around
collecting milk.'

A MERRY CHRISTMAS

'We did have
a Christmas tree.
We decorated it
on Christmas Eve.'

PEARS' ANNUAL 1913 6ᵈ

CONTENTS
12 HUMOROUS TALES
WITH

'We went to church at midnight.'

'We put up a sprig
of mistletoe as well.'

'We hung our stockings on the mantlepiece.
We always got an orange, a lump of coal,
a walnut, a sweet and something useful,
like a comb or a pencil.'

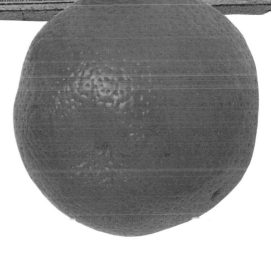

A PRESENT FOR A GOOD CHILD

'We usually had
one wrapped present each.
Sometimes we got clothes.
My most precious present
was a doll with a china head.'

1975

1950

Great-granny said,

'Food shops had
special displays
at Christmas.'

'Butchers hung rows and rows
of turkeys and geese outside their shops.'

'Grocers made special Christmas displays.'

'Up at the big house
where Dad worked as coachman,
they made a big to-do of Christmas.'

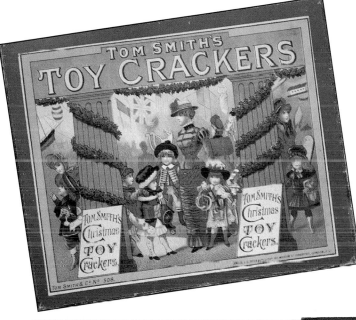

'Everyone dressed
in their best clothes.
They had a big Christmas tree
and crackers with their
Christmas dinner.'

'After Christmas, we had fun sticking cards
and scraps into an album to keep.'

27

Things to do

Look at these Christmas cards.
What Christmas traditions do they show?
Design your own Christmas card.

A Christmas Card with my love

Which of these things do you have
in your house at Christmas?
Find out whether they are the same
as the things your parents
and grandparents had
when they were children.

merry
christmas

Index

Photographs: Advertising Archives 11tl, 11tr, 19br; Barnaby's Picture Library 12c, 18bl; Camera Press 10bl, 13b; Bruce Coleman Ltd 24br; Mary Evans Picture Library 28tl; thanks to the Everyman Theatre, Cheltenham 17t; Robert Harding Picture Library 30 inset; Hulton Deutsch endpapers, cover tr, 16b, 18t, 20b, 21t; Billie Love Historical Collection 25b; Peter Millard cover br, title pg tr & b, imprint pg, 4-5, 6-7, 8-9, 10t, 10br, 11b, 12br, 14, 15t, 15br, 16tl, 16tr, 18br, 19tl, 21bl, 25t, 27b, 30-31; Robert Opie Collection 15bc, 21br, 22tr, 23t, 25tc, 27t; Picturepoint cover tl, cover bl, 13t, 15bl, 24t, 24bl; Popperfoto title pg tl, 17b, 19tr, 20t, 22b, 23b; Ruth Thomson 12tr, 14cr; thanks to J Sainsbury Archive 26.